Just Behind The Door

A collection of emotional poems

Cheyenne Blanchard

BookLeaf Publishing

India | USA | UK

Made with ❤ on the BookLeaf Publishing Platform
www.bookleafpub.in
www.bookleafpub.com

Dedication

I'd like to dedicate this book to first my found family, I never would have had the courage to even think about getting a book published without you. Second, I'd like to thank my wonderful partner for standing by me in every way and encouraging my writing, you're the best.

Preface

These poems are a collection of emotions I've experienced throughout my life. From loneliness to joy, feel free to feel your own feelings while you read them. This book is an open invitation to look into the shadows behind the mask you might wear on a day-to-day basis. Things like love, loss, heartbreak and even new experiences are referenced in this book.

Acknowledgements

I want to thank my friends for keeping me upright as I work through old thought patterns and traumas, my partner for doing everything they can to keep me writing, and finally my late grandma for showing art, love, and feelings of all forms. You all have taught me that I'm more than my traumas and brought me back to who I really am, for that I will forever be in your debt.

1. I'm Uncomfortable

Toss and turn

Toss and turn

Never sleeping just

Toss and turn

Remember who everyone forced you to be?

toss

Remember when you did that one thing? Gee

and

What about when you had that impulse?

turn

You're a joke

Toss

You're a fake

and

You're nothing

turn

Oh, you're cold?

grab the blanket then

but all you'll be able to do is

toss

and
turn

2

2. Love Songs

Every love song that I hear reminds me of you.

Too bad none of them will ever be enough to make you think of me first

3. Deafening Silence

How many times must we endure the silence?
The clock ticks
The music plays
But the silence stays

Doors slam

Voices yell

But nothing is louder than the silence
I should hear an apology
But the silence drags on

I miss the sounds

I miss the laughter

I miss the kisses

I miss when people were wrong about you

But now I face the consequences
Of trusting who you're supposed to be
Instead of who you really are.

4. Just You

Watching you get ready
I can't help but feel
The world is different
The world is real

Dancing around the kitchen
Laughing the entire way
This is a new dawn
This is a new day

5. Little Hands

Lost in the trauma
Of who I used to be
I can't differentiate
Between my adult self
and a child in pajamas

Your seething words
Cut her so deep
This child in pajamas
Who just can't sleep

She reaches out
Her tiny arms
Every time
There's a message

The adult me watches
With careful eyes
Knowing what could happen
Knowing it isn't wise

And yet she still reaches out
Tears in her eyes
Crying for her parents
Who never answered "why?"

6. Moving Forward

Old pictures
Old memories
Old friends
Old places
Old smells
Old feelings

I shed them away
Hoping for new

New friends
New feelings
New smells
New pictures
New places

It's all fun finding new things
While I grieve the old
Shedding the skin
Of who I've been

7. Mirror talk

Days are easier
Life is brighter
All because you exist
So stay
If not for yourself
For the colors you have yet to see
For the songs you haven't heard
For The temperatures you haven't complained about
For the food you haven't tasted
Stay
For the things and feelings you haven't experienced

8. Stuck in My Head

I hear you say
"Everything is fine."
But suddenly I'm deaf
I can only hear my mind

You show me
More beyond my cage
Suddenly I'm blind
I can only see the walls in my rage

I feel your touch
As you hug the tears away
Suddenly I'm numb
No feeling on this day

You reassure me
When the nightmares come crawling back
Suddenly it's dark
Any warmth I lack

The feelings come
They go and return
You're so patient
And full of concern

I'm just in my head
These cells I've called home
I'm not used
To leaving this dome

9. Unforgivable

"Forgive your parents"
Why should I?
For them it was a Tuesday
For me all year I cried

"But she's your mother"
But what about me?
For her it was a Wednesday
For me it was a trauma spree

"You forgave your father."
Why wouldn't I?
He accepted his negligence
Apologizing with his reasons why

"Just get over it."
Why is it that simple?
I replay those moments day after day
In my brain it's a never ending ripple

"You just hold grudges."
Wouldn't you?
I spent years in hell
In pain I walked through

"You're never satisfied."
Would you be?
I watched her love other kids
Begging for that to be me

10. Family Fractures

I wonder what it would've been like
To watch our family fall apart
I hope you are oblivious
To our family blight

I wish you were here
To comfort me
And support me
While I lose what I held dear

I wonder if you'd hear what I have to say
If you'd be as closed minded
Our family seems to think so
Would you also throw my feelings away?

I wish you were here
To listen
And cry
Feel our hearts clear

I wonder what you'd say
Knowing that I'm the way I am
Our family says you'd shun me
Not give me the time of day

I wish you were here
To prove them wrong
And show them their mistake
But they're too far gone I fear

I wonder if you hear me
Way up there somewhere
Our family says it's useless
But I know I can't agree

11. A Different Holiday

Turkeys cooked
Stuffing is mixed
Good smells in the air
Something's amiss

There's no screaming
No snide remarks
Just giggles and food
In our eyes a spark

The silence is comfortable
No awkward stare
Just love and smiles
Even laughter and care

I'm glad I'm here
Basking in these comforts
It should have always been this way
Our family should have come first

12. Wishing on Mobiles

Diapers in the corner
Toys strewn about the room
Problems I always wanted
but here I feel like a foreigner

Crying in the car
Tantrums in the store
Comfort I want to give
but never got that far

Lessons about life
Guidence galore
All these things to give
this is my strife

Empty cribs
Dust collecting on clothes
The pain of something that never was
a dull ache in my ribs

13. Thinking of You

I try to write
to find the words to describe
you

your smile
your laughter
your eyes

but somehow the words fall short

You bring everyone around joy
your laughter contagious
I hang on to your every word
like a child with a new toy

I want you to know
How
amazing
funny
adorable

loveable

but again, words fall short

It's not for lack of thought
I could write a whole book
but it'd be for naught
as you are more than simple words
written beautifully on a page

14. Christmas Blues

Christmas lights on the house
tree in the corner
cold in the air
Presents in the closet
Carols in the car
A voice is missing
A voice gone far

Joy in the kitchen
Laughter in the hall
Wrapping paper in the room
But I'm wrapping them alone
Instead of with you
Your cakes aren't in the oven
Your name not under the tree
Another Christmas we'll have
But you were the key

The family gathers
An empty seat at the table

It's never the same
Without your giggles
Without your warmth
Now we sit in the cold
And ignore each other

15. My Worries

Sometimes I worry
That the past will suck you back
Ripping you away from me
Because of something I lack
Sometimes I worry
My past will bleed me dry
Ripping us apart
Without even having to try

16. Dreaming

Watching you sleep
I can't help but dream
Though I'm wide awake
My daydreams run deep
I see the campground
The one we call home
An expensive black dress
Our friends all around
I see an apartment
Though it might not be much
We call it home
No complaints in that department
I see holidays
All around a table
Laughter and joy
Even jokes if we're able
You're still asleep
I'm wide awake
Dreaming about our future
Smiling without a peep

17. The Troubles With Faith

Sitting in the pews
The gospel music reverberates in me
The message never forgotten
The word no longer new

I feel like a stranger
In this shiny cathedral
Outfitted with Christmas lights
And trees and the like

Emotions bubble up
Tears threaten to flow
What is this feeling?
Leaving me colder than snow

I am a stranger
To this faith I once cherished
To this beautiful manger scene
I feel a sense of loneliness
Where I once have been

What would this have become?
Where would this path have led me?
This familiar ache within my soul
Makes me feel what I chose was dumb

I know who I am
I know what I believe
But sometimes I miss
The feelings the church would bring

18. Next Time

You worry after this life
what our next will be like
But I know I will always find you
My soul knows yours
Like the back of my hand
If you become a star
I'll be the astronomer
If you became an animal
I'd become your caretaker
If you became a drop in the ocean
I'd spend eternity drowning to find you
So don't worry my love
Any life I'll find you again
Without a doubt

19. Your Favorite

I wish I knew
What it was like
To be in your graces
My entire life

I wish I knew
How it felt
To be your favorite
No shitty hand dealt

All I know
Is the anger I feel
For being left behind
Constantly the bad deal

All I know
Are the wounds you gave
Treating me like nothing
Pushing me in a cave

20. Fire Mantra

It's fine
It's fine
It's fine
I continue to eat your words
Scalding my throat
Burning the hope
It's fine
It's fine
It's fine
Just keep breathing through the flames
Crying through the smoke
Just keep breathing
Don't choke

21. Steps

I watch you walk away
Your back turned
Each step further from me
Crying, screaming for you to stay
But you never stop
Since I was 7
Your back has been turned
Each step further from me
The child begging and pleading
The teen throwing and screaming
But now I no longer see it
My back turned
Each step closer to freedom
To those who love me
For who I am
Your crying and screaming
Falling on deaf ears